How Can I Live by Faith?

Crucial Questions booklets provide a quick introduction to definitive Christian truths. This expanding collection includes titles such as:

Who Is Jesus?

Can I Trust the Bible?

Does Prayer Change Things?

Can I Know God's Will?

How Should I Live in This World?

What Does It Mean to Be Born Again?

Can I Be Sure I'm Saved?

What Is Faith?

What Can I Do with My Guilt?

What Is the Trinity?

TO BROWSE THE REST OF THE SERIES,
PLEASE VISIT: **REFORMATIONTRUST.COM/CQ**

CQ

How Can
I Live
by Faith?

R.C. SPROUL

IR *Reformation Trust* A DIVISION OF LIGONIER MINISTRIES, ORLANDO, FL

How Can I Live by Faith?
© 2020 by R.C. Sproul

Published by Reformation Trust Publishing
a division of Ligonier Ministries
421 Ligonier Court, Sanford, FL 32771
Ligonier.org   ReformationTrust.com

Printed in China
RR Donnelley
0000620
First edition

ISBN 978-1-64289-237-6 (Paperback)
ISBN 978-1-64289-238-3 (ePub)
ISBN 978-1-64289-239-0 (Kindle)

Cover design: Ligonier Creative
Interior typeset: Katherine Lloyd, The DESK

Library of Congress Cataloging-in-Publication Data

Names: Sproul, R. C. (Robert Charles), 1939-2017, author.
Title: How can I live by faith? / R.C. Sproul.
Description: Orlando, FL : Reformation Trust Publishing, a division of
  Ligonier Ministries, 2020. | Series: Crucial questions; 35
Identifiers: LCCN 2019033744 (print) | LCCN 2019033745 (ebook) |
  ISBN 9781642892376 (paperback) | ISBN 9781642892383 (epub) |
  ISBN 9781642892390 (kindle edition)
Subjects: LCSH: Faith and reason--Christianity. | Faith. | Justification
  (Christian theology)
Classification: LCC BT50 .S67 2020 (print) | LCC BT50 (ebook) | DDC
  234/.23--dc23
LC record available at https://lccn.loc.gov/2019033744
LC ebook record available at https://lccn.loc.gov/2019033745

Contents

Chapter One

The Faithful God

The Christian faith is a reasonable faith. When we speak of "the Christian faith," in one sense, we mean the body of teachings that has been passed down by the prophets and Apostles and set authoritatively in sacred Scripture (Jude 3). But we also mean the center of a life based on that body of teaching, for at the center of the Christian life is faith. The essential meaning of faith is trust. To believe is to trust something or someone. This means that our personal reliance, what we hold on to, what we base our life on, is based on trusting something. Trust in God, faith in Christ alone for salvation, is at the center of the Christian religion, and it is a key part of the Christian life to learn how to live out that trust in a life of faith.

Since the Enlightenment of the eighteenth century, faith as a virtue has come under assault. The guns of intellectual criticism have been trained on our faith as the self-anointed intellectuals have positioned faith as utterly opposed to rationality, as inherently irrational. As a result, many Christians have retreated from the arena of debate. Not only that, they've gone further and concluded that rationality and reason are tools of Satan that contradict the truth of Christ.

The pernicious influence of Enlightenment-era rationality has even worked its way into the church. The theological liberalism of the nineteenth century brought an assault against the basic foundational views of the Christian faith. This theological movement progressed into the twentieth and twenty-first centuries to basic unbelief and has taken hold of many church institutions. Some Christian parents have even found that upon sending their children off to ostensibly Christian colleges and universities, their children come back filled with doubts and skepticism propagated by the very professors the church had entrusted to teach and explain the faith.

In our day, thanks to the influence of the Enlightenment and the attacks of theological liberalism, many people see a sharp divorce between faith and reason. In fact, we are living in the most anti-intellectual period in the history of the Christian church. What noted biblical archaeologist William Foxwell Albright called "a baleful influence of existential philosophy" has permeated not only secular culture but also Christian culture so much that we have now become suspicious of reason. As a result, many people today believe that rationality and intellect have little to do with religion or faith. Some feel uncomfortable even talking about categories of logic because they have been steeped in the idea that Christianity is to be embraced by faith and not by reason.

The reaction against this tendency was to move away from intellectualism under the dual false assumptions that intellectualism leads to unbelief and that Christians must live by faith and not by reason. As a result, the concept of faith that has emerged is often prefaced by the word *blind*. How many times have you heard people say that we must accept something by faith? Perhaps you've said something similar. But what if someone responded by asking, "*Why should I take it by faith?*" In other words, should we ask people to believe by blind faith for no reason whatsoever except our own personal assertion? Isn't blind faith nothing more than asking someone to believe something simply because we said so? And if that's the case, why should anyone believe us over someone else?

As believers, we owe people answers to these questions. When we seek to give answers, we find ourselves engaged in apologetics. If we proclaim the message of the gospel of Christ, warn people that their ultimate destiny depends on their response to His claims, and then tell them to simply take it on blind faith, we do violence to God the Father, who is the fountainhead of all truth. We do violence to God the Son, who is the incarnation of truth. And we do violence to God the Holy Ghost, who is the Spirit of truth.

If I trust someone who is not trustworthy, that's superstition and foolishness. So the basic answer of the apologist, when asked why someone should trust God, is because God is trustworthy. Of course, we must also demonstrate to people that God is trustworthy. To be a Christian is to live by trusting God with our life and our death. Why do we do that?

To answer that question, we'll look to my favorite chapter in the whole Bible—Genesis 15. Verses 1 and 2 say: "After these things the word of the LORD came to Abram in a vision: 'Fear not, Abram, I am your shield; your reward shall be very great.' But Abram said, 'O Lord GOD, what will you give me, for I continue childless, and the heir of my house is Eliezer of Damascus?'"

To set the context for the story, Abraham has been called out of Ur of the Chaldeans, and he is apprehensive. He's experiencing a crisis of faith with the little bit of faith that he possesses. In this moment, God comes to him and says, "Fear not." The Christian life is a life of faith, and a life of faith means a life of trust. There's no commandment given by God that is more difficult to obey than this one.

This command occurs about a hundred times more than the second most repeated command. When God calls people, He says, "Fear not." When angels appear, they say, "Fear not." When Jesus appears, He often says, "Fear not." Why is this? Do you think that perhaps He knows something about us? Perhaps the greatest danger to the Christian church is the paralysis that comes from fear.

When God appears to Abraham, the first thing He says is "Fear not, Abram, I am your shield." An existentialist, who believes that life is meaningless and the ultimate destiny is absolute annihilation in the pit of nonbeing, would say that we ought not to fear but instead ought to be authentic, courageous people who take life by the horns. Fear not; life is meaningless, he would say. But that line of thinking is insane.

God's reasoning is very different. When God says "Fear not," the reason not to be afraid follows: because "I am your shield." During His earthly ministry, Jesus put it this way: "But take heart; I have overcome the world" (John 16:33). The existentialist would say, "Be of good cheer; the world will overcome you." When God calls Abraham to respond with faith, He gives him a reason that makes sense—because "I am your shield." If God is our shield, would it be reasonable or unreasonable to be paralyzed by fear? If we knew God was shielding us, what would that do to our fear? We could do anything if we really believed that God was our shield.

Then, God goes further by saying, "Your reward shall be very great" (Gen. 15:1). Abraham must have wondered at this statement, for at this point, he was childless, and in ancient Near Eastern culture, having a son to take the inheritance was crucial. He voices this concern when he says, "O Lord GOD, what will you give me, for I continue childless, and the heir of my house is Eliezer of Damascus?" and "Behold, you have given me no offspring, and a member of my household will be my heir" (vv. 2–3).

Abraham is asking God what He could possibly give him to compensate for the fact that he has no son. The Lord responds: "'This man shall not be your heir; your very own son shall be your heir.' And he brought him outside and said, 'Look toward heaven, and number the stars, if you are able to number them.' Then he said to him, 'So shall your offspring be'" (vv. 4–5).

Have you ever tried to number the stars? In this passage in Genesis, Abraham is outside his tent on a starry night gazing up at the Milky Way galaxy, brilliant and clear. Amid billions of stars, Abraham looks up and attempts to count them. God tells Abraham that not only would he have an heir, but that his heirs would be as numerous as the stars of the sky and the sand of the sea. And in verses 6–7 we read: "And he believed the LORD, and he counted it to him as righteousness. And he said to him, 'I am the LORD who brought you out from Ur of the Chaldeans to give you this land to possess.'"

Right after God pronounced Abraham justified by

faith, Abraham—this father of the faithful—says, "O Lord GOD, how am I to know that I shall possess it?" (v. 8). We might expect God to lose patience with Abraham at this point. Had He not just said He would give Abraham an heir? God is immutably, eternally truthful. The Lord God has no shadow of turning in Him. He does not break His promises. He does whatever He says He will do. But God recognizes that Abraham is struggling to live by faith and trust that God would do what He said He would do. So He answers Abraham's question by giving him an unforgettable experience.

> He said to him, "Bring me a heifer three years old, a female goat three years old, a ram three years old, a turtledove, and a young pigeon." And he brought him all these, cut them in half, and laid each half over against the other. But he did not cut the birds in half. And when birds of prey came down on the carcasses, Abram drove them away.
>
> As the sun was going down, a deep sleep fell on Abram. And behold, dreadful and great darkness fell upon him. Then the LORD said to Abram, "Know for certain that your offspring will be sojourners in

a land that is not theirs and will be servants there, and they will be afflicted for four hundred years. But I will bring judgment on the nation that they serve, and afterward they shall come out with great possessions. As for you, you shall go to your fathers in peace; you shall be buried in a good old age. And they shall come back here in the fourth generation, for the iniquity of the Amorites is not yet complete." (vv. 9–16)

And then, the verse of all verses: "When the sun had gone down and it was dark, behold, a smoking fire pot and a flaming torch passed between these pieces" (v. 17). It's possible to read this verse a thousand times and still miss what's happening. What is described in this verse provides the historical basis for why a Christian can live by faith.

In the Old Testament, the expression for when a covenant was instituted between people was to say the covenant was *cut* rather than *made*. This expression was illustrated vividly in the rite of circumcision (Gen. 17), where Abraham and his household and descendants were commanded to cut off the foreskins of their flesh as a way of marking themselves as God's people, as those who were in covenant with Him.

This rite had a symbolic meaning with both a positive and negative element. The positive meaning symbolized being cut off from the wickedness and evil of the world and being consecrated unto God, just as the skin had been cut off. The negative element was this: the recipient of circumcision was saying to God in graphic terms that if he didn't obey the terms of the covenant, he would be cut off from God's presence and all the benefits that flow from being in relationship with Him. He would be cut out and cast into outer darkness from the kingdom of God and His beloved Son, just as he had cut off the foreskin of his flesh. That was dramatic.

In Genesis 15:17, we read of the circumcision not of Abraham but of God. God instructed Abraham to get the animals, cut them in half, and lay them out with half on one side and half on the other. Then, a horrible darkness fell on Abraham. In the midst of this darkness, he saw "a smoking fire pot and a flaming torch." He saw this fire burning and flickering and flaming, and then the flame began to move through the pieces.

What was the smoking fire pot and the flaming torch? Or perhaps more accurately, *who* was the smoking fire pot and the flaming torch? What we have in verse 17 is a theophany—a visible manifestation of the invisible God, who often appeared in the Old Testament embodied visibly in the mode of fire. The burning bush, the pillar of fire, the consuming fire, is God Himself (see Ex. 3:2; 13:21; Lev. 10:2). What Abraham saw was God passing through these pieces. God was saying this to Abraham: "If there's one promise to you and to your seed that I fail to keep, may I, the Lord God Omnipotent, be as these animals. May My divine being be cut in half. May the immutable God suffer mutation. May the indivisible God be divided. May the infinite God be fragmented." That's what God was saying.

On that day, God said to Abraham—and to all who would come after Abraham—that He keeps His promises, and He swore by the integrity of His own being. Have you ever taken an oath? As children, we say, "Cross my heart and hope to die, stick a needle in my eye." Or perhaps we swear on another's grave. We say crazy things to emphasize to people that they can trust us, that we will keep our promises. Or perhaps as adults, we've sworn in a courtroom with our hand on the Bible vowing to "tell the truth, the whole truth, and nothing but the truth."

Blind faith? God forbid. Our God is utterly trustworthy. People will risk their possessions, their reputations, and perhaps even their lives for us. But God risks His eternal being. He has pledged His eternal being; all that He is and all that He has, He has put on the line as a surety for His promise. To not believe Him is irrational.

Chapter Two

Redeemed by Faith

The cardinal doctrine of the Protestant Reformation was the doctrine of justification by faith alone. And the classic biblical text that lays the foundation for this doctrine is found in Paul's letter to the church at Rome. Martin Luther, while a professor at Wittenberg, Germany, was preparing lectures on Romans for his seminary students when he experienced a burst of understanding into the meaning of this letter.

As an Augustinian monk and a dutiful disciple, Luther

was reading an essay penned by Augustine of Hippo more than a thousand years earlier. As Luther read, suddenly light dawned on his mind and soul, and he understood clearly the doctrine of justification by faith alone. He later recalled that at that moment, it was as if the doors of paradise swung open and he walked through. This was a key moment in church history.

Of course, the first one to explain the doctrine of justification by faith alone was not Martin Luther or Augustine. The doctrine was first spelled out in detail by the Apostle Paul in the book of Romans. In the first two chapters of this letter, Paul has declared the universality of human sinfulness that has brought all mankind, Jew and Greek, before the tribunal of God.

Then, in 3:19, he says, "Now we know that whatever the law says it speaks to those who are under the law, so that every mouth may be stopped, and the whole world may be held accountable to God." When Jesus speaks of the final judgment, and when the New Testament writers speak of that final tribunal, we see a consistent description of the human reaction to the charges leveled against us by God. That reaction is silence. When God delivers an indictment, the mouths of men are stopped. Time has run out for excuses and attempts at self-justification. Before the throne of God, a guilty world is silent.

Then comes the Apostolic conclusion: "For by works of the law no human being will be justified in his sight, since through the law comes knowledge of sin" (v. 20). We see the law of God, and by measuring ourselves against the law, we know that we do not measure up. The bad news is that the whole world is guilty and no one will be justified through the works of the law.

Then comes the single greatest word in all of Scripture. Verse 21 introduces what we have come to call the gospel, the good news of Christ. It's a three-letter word, and in and of itself it seems insignificant. Yet it is the word upon which our eternal destinies hang—the word *but*. After receiving the bad news of the severity of God's indictment against humanity, the Scriptures pause and say:

> But now the righteousness of God has been manifested apart from the law, although the Law and the Prophets bear witness to it—the righteousness of God through faith in Jesus Christ for all who believe. For there is no distinction: for all have sinned and fall short of the glory of God, and are justified by

his grace as a gift, through the redemption that is in Christ Jesus, whom God put forward as a propitiation by his blood, to be received by faith. This was to show God's righteousness, because in his divine forbearance he had passed over former sins. It was to show his righteousness at the present time, so that he might be just and the justifier of the one who has faith in Jesus. (vv. 21–26)

God is altogether righteous and perfectly holy. He is a just God, and His law reflects His righteousness. He justly demands of us perfect obedience to His just and righteous law, but we do not obey that law. That provokes a dilemma. If God is a just God, what does He do with unjust people? Some in the church today may never have even considered that problem. It seems that in the present-day Christian community, there is a presumption of mercy and grace. And the glory of the gospel has been eclipsed because people assume the grace of God. Therefore, there's nothing amazing about God's grace toward us. Yet the question remains: How can God maintain His justice and still be the justifier?

Some wrongly assume that all God has to do to save a fallen humanity is overlook our sin and simply grant forgiveness unilaterally, graciously, and mercifully. After all, if humans can do that for each other, why can't God? However, it's one thing for a sinner to forgive another sinner. But God is perfectly just and holy, and He cannot and will not ever negotiate His own integrity and righteousness. So if He is just and must maintain that justice, what does He do with unjust people?

Through justification, God can be both just *and* the justifier of the one who believes in Jesus. Paul tells us the result: "Then what becomes of our boasting? It is excluded. By what kind of law? By a law of works? No, but by the law of faith. For we hold that one is justified by faith apart from works of the law" (vv. 27–28).

In this text, Paul has told us that all people are sinners. He's also said that no one can be justified through the works of the law. If we can't be justified through the works of the law, either we can't be justified at all or we must be justified some other way. Paul then tells us that we are justified by a righteousness that is not our own. It is an alien righteousness, a foreign righteousness. It is someone else's righteousness. It is the righteousness of Jesus, and Jesus' righteousness becomes the basis for our justification. We are not just in ourselves, but Jesus is just.

If you asked a child in the church what Jesus did for him, the child would likely say, "Jesus died on the cross for my sins." Our children understand that. But that's only half of what is involved in justification. To be justified demands not only that our sins be punished (the negative dimension) but also that we possess positive righteousness to present before God. If we are to be justified, we must both get rid of our unjustness and acquire justice. These two things must happen, and the gospel says that both are provided by Christ.

On the one hand, our unjustness is applied to Jesus. When Jesus died on the cross, He died for our sins, to pay the punishment for our wickedness. But again, that's only half of what is needed. The other half happens when, at the moment we place our trust in Jesus, His righteousness is transferred to our account before God. Jesus takes our unrighteousness and gives us His righteousness in the sight of God. As a result, God can remain both just and merciful. Why is He just? Because He has actually given us the righteousness of Christ. God declares people—who in and of themselves are unrighteous—righteous after He has clothed them and covered them with the righteousness of Christ. On the cross, He declared Christ unrighteous and accursed and punished our sin in Him. It is a double transfer that can take place only through trusting in Christ.

Therefore, for a Christian to live by faith means not only to trust God the Father but also to trust God the Son alone for our justification. Justification by faith alone means that justification is by Christ alone. The only way that we as unjust people can stand in the presence of a just God is if we have righteousness. If we are unjust, we obviously do not have righteousness on our own, so it must come from outside of us. We must either get it from Christ or, in an exercise of futility, attempt to get it somewhere else.

Nothing angers Americans more than the claim that there's only one way to God—through Jesus. People think it's unfair, bigoted, and narrow-minded. The implied criticism is directed against God, the idea being that God has not done enough to make redemption possible. Can you imagine a sinner standing before God at the end of the age and criticizing Him for not doing enough to provide for our salvation, for not allowing all people to be saved or for not allowing people to be saved in a variety of ways? Should God allow people to be saved by trusting in the Buddha, for instance?

The problem is that the Buddha doesn't have enough righteousness to save himself, let alone to save us. Confucius, too, fell short of the glory of God. There's only One who has met the job description necessary to make our justification possible. Does anyone want to argue for the sinlessness of Moses? The sinlessness of Muhammad? The biggest difference between Christianity and every other religion is the atonement of Jesus Christ and the perfect righteousness of Jesus Christ. We lose sight of that when we want to be so broad-minded that we affirm the truth of different religions, but what we're really saying is that it's all right for God to negotiate His righteousness. We want God to be the justifier, and we don't particularly care whether He remains just.

"For we hold that one is justified by faith apart from works of the law" (Rom. 3:28). A person is justified by Christ and by Christ alone. That's a nutshell summary of the Protestant doctrine of justification by faith alone. The Protestant Reformation was, of course, a serious matter, for it is a serious matter to divide the body of Christ. It was so serious that our Lord prayed with His disciples in earnest that all His followers would be unified. He prayed to His Father regarding us, "that they may be one even as we are one" (John 17:22). God the Father and God the Son have an intense union, so Jesus' prayer that we would have that same kind of unity—not just a superficial unity, but a profound unity—was remarkable. Therefore, to rupture the body of Christ is serious indeed.

But Luther said that the issue of how a person is redeemed is the article upon which the church stands or falls. Moreover, it is the article by which we stand or fall. If justification is by faith alone, what happens to the person who is not trusting in Christ and Christ alone for his salvation? What if he is trusting in his works? What if he is trusting partly in works and partly in Christ? The question naturally arises: Is such a person really placing his confidence and reliance and trust in Christ who alone can save him?

The issue isn't structures of authority, church government, or organization. The debate isn't over rituals or sacraments. It's over salvation. Is it by faith alone or through some mixture of faith and something else? We often hear that the Roman Catholic Church believes in justification by works and the Protestants believe in justification by faith. But that's not true. That's a distortion of Roman Catholic theology, and it's slanderous, because Rome has always taught that faith is required. However, it also teaches that good works are required for salvation.

Neither the Roman Catholic nor the Protestant view of justification is the dominant view of the American culture today. The most prevalent view of justification is one that we might call justification by death. This idea states that all someone has to do to get into heaven is die. It doesn't matter what someone believes as long as he is sincere. All God requires is that people believe *something*. If all one has to do to get to heaven is die, then why should we become exercised about correct doctrine or truth or anything else? We're all going to get there anyway because everyone goes to heaven.

This idea did not originate from Christianity. It did not come from Paul. It did not come from Jesus. And it did not come from God. In this view, there's no need for Christ. There's no need to repent. There's no need for putting one's personal trust in Christ and clinging to Him for justification. People don't get excited about justification anymore, so we wrongly believe that we have become mature because we no longer fight over religion. We don't burn people at the stake; we don't throw people into prison. After years of fighting between Roman Catholics and Protestants, we say that we're going to make peace and not fight anymore.

But do you know what kind of people never fight about religion? People who don't care about religion. People who never argue about Christ are people who don't care about

Christ. People who never argue about the most crucial question before the human race are those who don't care about the most crucial question before the human race—namely, how an unjust person will ever be able to stand before a just and holy God.

When Luther walked through the doors of paradise, he did not want to slam them shut and stay in paradise by himself. He wanted to swing that door open, paint a picture on top of the door, and say to the whole world: "Here's the gospel! Hear the gospel! Understand the gospel! Put your faith in Christ, and you will be justified." But his doctrine was not received by the church, and the pope excommunicated Luther.

Rome ultimately responded to the Protestant Reformation at the Council of Trent in the middle of the sixteenth century. There, the Roman Catholic Church declared that anyone who believes that justification is by faith alone—meaning that all one had to do was place his personal trust in Christ and in Christ alone for salvation—is anathema, or damned. In this dark hour, the church condemned anyone who believed the gospel.

That's why Luther was willing to splinter the church. Luther was ready to die for the gospel because he was ready to die for his Savior. At the Council of Trent, Rome responded not only by condemning Luther and the Reformation but also by declaring its own doctrine of justification. It turned to the book of James to find a biblical basis for its view: "Was not Abraham our father justified by works when he offered up his son Isaac on the altar? . . . You see that a person is justified by works and not by faith alone" (James 2:21, 24).

Luther said that a person is justified by faith alone. But James said that a person is justified by works and *not* by faith alone. What are we to make of this seeming contradiction? Do we believe Luther or the Bible? In the book of James, we see a positive affirmation—"a person is justified by works"; we also see a denial—"and not by faith alone."

The situation looks even more grim when we consider who James is using as an example in his teaching of justification by works: Abraham. Paul states in Romans 4:1–5:

What then shall we say was gained by Abraham, our forefather according to the flesh? For if Abraham was justified by works, he has something to boast about, but not before God. For what does the Scripture say? "Abraham believed God, and it was counted to him as righteousness." Now to the one who works, his wages are not counted as a gift but as his due. And to the one who does not work but believes in him who justifies the ungodly, his faith is counted as righteousness.

Who is the Apostle Paul's exhibit A to prove his argument that justification is not by the works of the law but by faith alone? Abraham. He is the father of the faithful, and we must be justified in the same way that Abraham was justified. But then James also says to look at Abraham. Abraham was justified by his works. Do you see the problem?

New Testament theologians and exegetes have extensively considered this seeming contradiction, and they have proposed various solutions. Some scholars argue that Paul wrote Romans first, before James was written. In this view, James was written after Romans to correct the Apostle Paul's teaching of justification.

Another theory is that James was written before Romans, and that James, though he lived with Jesus and listened to his brother teach and preach, never really heard the message. As a result, James was the first heretic to teach justification by works, so the Apostle Paul wrote Romans to counteract the deleterious influence of James' epistle.

Both of these views raise serious questions about the integrity of Paul, James, and ultimately the canon of the New Testament. Is it possible without special pleading to reconcile these two viewpoints?

First, we must ask what James is concerned with in his epistle. We must look earlier in chapter 2 at verse 14, which says, "What good is it, my brothers, if someone says he has faith but does not have works? Can that faith save him?" James is addressing this question: Is justification by faith or by a *profession* of faith? It is possible for a person to make a profession of faith and not have faith. We should not assume that all those who join the visible church—the community of those who have professed faith in Christ, along with their children—are truly regenerate people who are placing their trust and confidence in Christ and Christ alone.

Does not our Lord Himself teach that many will come to Him on the last day saying, "Lord, Lord"? And He will say, "I never knew you; depart from me, you workers of lawlessness" (Matt. 7:21, 23). He also said of His own generation, "This people honors me with their lips, but their heart is far from me" (Matt. 15:8). He told us that there would always be tares growing along with the wheat—people who say they believe but are not true believers (Matt. 13:24–30).

In fact, if our understanding of Scripture is correct, in all probability there are people in each visible church body who have openly declared their confidence and faith in Christ who in fact are not in the kingdom of God because they're not trusting in Christ for their salvation. They're trusting in their own good works, or their own righteousness, or how many times they've gone to church. They really believe they will enter the kingdom of God by living a pretty good life. But these people are far from the kingdom of God.

The early church had to address this issue, and James does so very practically. He essentially asks: "What good is it? What does it profit a person if he says he has faith but has no works? What is the indispensable sign of true faith? Does it mean that I just believe Jesus died for me and I can live as wickedly as I want the rest of my days?" Jesus answered this very succinctly: "If you love me, you will keep my commandments" (John 14:15). Luther, understanding this, put it brilliantly: "We are justified by faith alone, but not by a faith that is alone." The kind of faith that saves us is a *fides viva*, a living faith, a vital faith, a faith that demonstrates itself in obedience.

We do not have to wait until we achieve good works before God declares us His. We are declared His at the moment we believe. This is the issue that Paul is dealing with as he labors the point that at the moment we believe in Christ, all that He has is ours. Through justification, we are free from condemnation, we have access to God, we are forgiven, and a true faith is alive in our hearts. That faith will begin to manifest itself in a changed life. The good news is that we don't have to achieve that life before God will receive us.

James, however, is dealing with a different issue—that of those who say they have faith but have no works. He basically asks, "Can that faith save them?" The answer is a resounding no. A faith that does not produce works is no faith. James goes on to call it a dead faith (James 2:26). It has no life to it. It profits nothing. It can save no one.

When James wants to show his readers what true faith is, he uses Abraham as his exhibit A: "Was not Abraham our father justified by works when he offered up his son Isaac on the altar?" (James 2:21). Both James and Paul appeal to Abraham, and they appeal to different times and different points in Abraham's life. James points to Genesis 22. In Romans 4, Paul points to Genesis 15, which we looked at in the last chapter, using it to argue that the moment Abraham believed God, he was justified.

Genesis 15 comes before Isaac was born or placed on the altar, before Abraham had done any of the works of the law. But when Abraham believed God and trusted His promises, God pronounced him righteous. According to Paul, Abraham was justified in Genesis 15. But James says that Abraham was justified when he offered Isaac on the altar—seven chapters *after* Abraham was justified according to Paul. It may seem as if the apparent contradiction is getting worse, but it isn't.

James and Paul are speaking of two different concepts. The unfortunate problem for us when we read the English translation of the Bible is that the same Greek word is used in both—*dikaiosynē*—and it is translated in both cases by the word *justify* or *justification*. But if we carefully examine the meaning of the word *dikaiosynē* in its Greek origin, we see that it carries at least three or four different meanings.

One meaning is to vindicate or show something to be what it claims to be. This is the meaning in view for James;

remember, he was dealing with people who claimed to have faith. Now if Abraham said he had faith and then he did works, then Abraham's works show, manifest, and vindicate his claim that he has true faith. That is, Abraham's profession of faith is justified by Abraham's performance of obedience. In this sense, Abraham is justified or vindicated before mankind, for it is through his works that people can see his faith.

Paul is thinking of justification in another sense. If someone claims to have faith, God does not have to wait and see what that person does to know whether his profession of faith is sincere. God can see the heart. As soon as a man truly believes, God knows it. He knows if that faith is sincere. He does not have to wait to see the fruit of a man's life over time to assess whether his faith is genuine. This is justification from God's perspective.

To understand this seeming contradiction between faith and works between Paul and James, it is critical to realize that the word *justify* is used in two different ways: with respect to our standing before God (Paul) and with respect to our estimation among men (James). What we call the theological meaning of justification is what Paul labors to explain in his epistle to the Romans. He explains how a person is justified in the sight of a just and holy God. James, however, speaks of how a person's profession of faith is justified in the sight of men.

Paul and James are talking on two completely different levels when it comes to the word *justification*. But the grand doctrine, the theological meaning of justification—that is, how an unjust person will ever survive in the sight of a holy and just God—is the theme of the Apostle Paul's teaching. Without compromise, without negotiation, Paul is declaring that a man is justified by faith in Christ and by faith in Christ alone. "For by works of the law no human being will be justified in his sight" (Rom. 3:20). To look to James to obscure the clear teaching of Paul is to completely misunderstand both Paul and James.

Our obedience to Christ will demonstrate that our profession of faith is genuine, but it is not the basis upon which we are saved. Even our best works are tainted by the abiding sin in our lives. The best work we can ever do cannot add an ounce of merit to the merit of the perfect righteousness of Jesus Christ. The issue is by whose merits we are saved. Is it through the merit of Jesus, through our own merit, or through the treasury of merits accumulated by the saints of the church?

The only authentic, intrinsic merit that has ever been earned in the sight of God was earned by Jesus, and so it is to Jesus that we fly. It is to Jesus that we cling, understanding that the life of faith means that the just shall live by faith (Rom. 1:17), by trusting in Christ and in Christ alone for our salvation. For He alone meets the requirements of a just and holy God.

God is both just and justifier. The marvelous truth of the gospel is that He transfers to us the righteousness of Christ and transfers to Christ our unrighteousness. His holy, righteous law is not compromised, and His justice remains intact. Yet at the very same time, He shows His mercy and grace.

Chapter Three

Dying
in Faith

In Christian circles, we often talk about what it means to live by faith. But what does it mean to die by faith? The patriarch Job asked, "If a man dies, shall he live again?" (Job 14:14). I doubt if there's any philosophical question that has attracted more practical interest than that question. The specter of death hangs over each one of us. It visits each of our homes, and we know that it awaits each one of us at some point.

The Bible teaches that the sting of death has been

removed, but it still remains an enemy—the final and most ferocious enemy. But as Christians, we have joined those in history who believed the initial proclamation of the first Christian church: "He is risen."

At the heart of the Christian faith stands the resurrected Christ, who said to His people: "I am the resurrection and the life. Whoever believes in me, though he die, yet shall he live" (John 11:25). This same Jesus said to His disciples: "In my Father's house are many rooms. If it were not so, would I have told you that I go to prepare a place for you?" (John 14:2). As Christians, we believe that death is not final. But the question we must raise is this: Is our faith in life after death a blind faith? Is it merely a projection of our own desires, the fulfillment of our own wishes? Is it simply a psychological fantasy? Or is there any sober reason why we believe in the triumph of Christ over death?

Philosophers have examined this question for ages. One of Plato's most famous dialogues, the *Phaedo*, narrates the death scene of Plato's beloved mentor, Socrates, who had been sentenced to death by drinking hemlock. Before he died, Socrates entered into a discussion with Plato about the question of life after death. Plato follows an intricate pattern of reasoning in which he looks to nature, noting its diversity. He notices the cyclical pattern of the world around us—how before a flower can bloom, first a seed must be placed in the ground. That seed, to germinate, must first decay. As it decays, it springs forth new life, and that new life produces seeds. After the flower withers and fades, the seeds filter back to the ground, and they decay and life comes again.

Plato says that as darkness follows daylight, and as the cycle of nature goes on, we see this pattern constantly repeating—generation, decay, generation. He points to the moth, the caterpillar, and the butterfly, showing how life goes through changes of form. With all this grandeur of change, all the diversity of forms of life that we see, Plato queries why we should expect our present form as intelligent human beings to be the highest or final form of life on this planet.

While Plato's thoughts are certainly interesting, they remain speculative. They do not provide compelling reasons to believe in life beyond death. They give us, at best, interesting analogies. Other philosophers have searched different avenues to examine the topic of life after death. Immanuel Kant wrote a massive treatise titled *Critique of Pure Reason*, which stands as the most comprehensive criticism of the traditional arguments for the existence of God. Kant ended his examination of apologetics and Christianity with a type of learned agnosticism in which he declared that through scientific inquiry we can have no conviction of the existence of God.

But after dismissing God from the front door of the house, Kant went around to the back door and tried to smuggle the deity back in through the kitchen by presenting what he called a moral argument for the existence of God. Kant argued for the existence of God not on theoretical grounds but strictly on practical and ethical grounds. According to Kant, in every human being resides an indelible sense of moral responsibility—that is, we all experience an internal imperative that commands our consciences. Though we may commit heinous crimes, we can never totally vanquish the remnants of conscience in our minds. We all have a sense of what is right and what is wrong.

Further, Kant argued that both individuals and society cannot function without some code of ethics. If society degenerated into a moral free-for-all, life would become not only chaotic but also impossible. Kant understood that there are people who don't always fulfill their selfish desires. Some people make sacrifices and do things simply because they are convinced that they are the right things to do. Kant asked why people would do that unless there is justice. In other words, for ethics to be meaningful, there must be justice.

This leads to the next question: What would have to be the case for justice to exist? We look around the world and see that sometimes justice does not prevail. Sometimes the wicked prosper and the righteous perish. Occasionally justice comes to pass, but justice in this world is clearly not perfect. So, why should a person be good if justice does not always prevail?

Kant would say that in order for justice to prevail ultimately (since it does not always prevail in this world), mankind must survive the grave. He saw life after death as a practical necessity for justice, and justice as a practical necessity for ethics to be meaningful. What else would have to be true for justice to prevail beyond surviving the grave? After all, there's no guarantee that surviving the grave secures justice. Perhaps in the next world there's as much injustice as there is on earth. In order to ensure that justice prevails ultimately, there must also be a judge. That judge, to ensure the ultimate victory of justice, must possess some necessary qualities.

First, the judge must be just. If the ultimate judge in the ultimate court were corrupt, then we would not have ultimate justice. The guarantee of ultimate justice requires not only a judge but a just judge. But even if there were a just judge, it would still not guarantee ultimate justice, because it's possible that the judge might make mistakes in his evaluation, however just and honorable he may be. So, Kant speculated that the ultimately just judge must also be omniscient, to ensure that all mitigating circumstances and necessary evidence appropriate to the trial would be brought to bear and perfectly analyzed, that perfect justice might prevail.

But even if there were an omnisciently perfect just judge, that *still* wouldn't guarantee justice, for even if his decisions were perfectly correct, how could we ensure that his decisions would be carried out? He would also require the power to enforce the verdict he declares. Therefore, that judge would need to be not only omniscient but also omnipotent. The deity Kant brought in through the back door sounds very much like Yahweh, the God of the Bible, whom he kicked out of the front door. His bottom line was this: We must live as if there was a God because if there is no God, then ethics are meaningless.

If there is no life after death, then ultimately all our ethical decisions are absolutely meaningless. This is the inescapable conclusion. The only alternative to an absolute ethic is a relative ethic. Humanism waxes eloquent about how important it is for us to be virtuous and to work for human dignity. But intellectually, there's nothing more pitiful than philosophical humanism, which tells us that our origin as human beings is a cosmic accident—that we are grown-up germs who have emerged fortuitously from the slime, and that we are destined ultimately to annihilation and nonbeing—but in between our origin and our destiny we enjoy enormous significance. Talk about fantasy and wish projection. Talk about blind faith and leaping into absurdity. What could be more absurd than to celebrate the significance of grown-up germs?

If we're going to care about human beings and human dignity, there should be a *reason* for that. If we are called to sacrificial, altruistic action on behalf of other human beings, we should have a good reason to act on that calling. It must be a better reason than simply arguing that we should be for people because we are people. For unless we can establish that it means something to be people, this way of thinking is pure emotion.

Those who followed Kant examined and challenged his argument. Friedrich Nietzsche, for example, criticized him for saying that we ought to believe in life after death and in God simply because if there is no God, then life is meaningless. If that's true, then we believe in God simply because we can't stand to think of our lives as insignificant and meaningless. That is inventing God simply because, from an emotional standpoint, we can't bear to live without Him. Instead, Nietzsche argued, we should face the existential truth that the bottom line of human existence is *das Nichtige*—nothingness.

Pessimistic existentialism came to the forefront and challenged the naivete of nineteenth-century humanism, asserting that it is not enough to argue for God simply because the alternatives to God's existence are grim. We can see in Western culture today the broad surrender to the meaninglessness of human existence and the philosophy of despair.

One of the most brilliant minds and greatest writers that this nation has ever produced is Edgar Allan Poe. He captured the cultural sense of despair more vividly and poignantly than perhaps anyone else. He did so in his magnificent poem "The Raven," which begins as follows:

Once upon a midnight dreary, while I pondered,
  weak and weary,
Over many a quaint and curious volume of
  forgotten lore—
    While I nodded, nearly napping, suddenly there
      came a tapping,
    As of some one gently rapping, rapping at my
      chamber door.
"'Tis some visitor," I muttered, "tapping at my
  chamber door—
      Only this and nothing more."

Ah, distinctly I remember it was in the bleak
  December;
And each separate dying ember wrought its ghost
  upon the floor.
    Eagerly I wished the morrow;—vainly I had
      sought to borrow
    From my books surcease of sorrow—sorrow for
      the lost Lenore—
For the rare and radiant maiden whom the angels
  name Lenore—
      Nameless *here* for evermore.

In this poem, a man is mourning a woman—his passion, his love—who has died. And the question of the poem is this: Is that one whom I loved gone forever, or will I see her again? A strange bird enters his chamber and croaks the refrain "Nevermore," which punctures the man's hopes and drives him into a frenzy. Through stanza after remorseful stanza, the terrible repetition of this reply from the fiendish bird moves the tormented man to scream in anger at his nocturnal visitor:

> "Prophet!" said I, "thing of evil!—prophet still, if
> bird or devil!—
> Whether Tempter sent, or whether tempest tossed
> thee here ashore,
> Desolate yet all undaunted, on this desert land
> enchanted—
> On this home by Horror haunted—tell me truly,
> I implore—
> Is there—*is* there balm in Gilead?—tell me—tell
> me, I implore!"
> Quoth the Raven "Nevermore."

That is the humanist answer to the greatest of all human dilemmas, the reality of death. A generation of thinkers said to Immanuel Kant: "It's not enough to wish for life after death. If all we have are wishes, then let us steel ourselves as men and face the mournful refrain of the raven—'Nevermore.'"

When we read the Apostolic response to this question, at first glance it seems as though what we read from the pen of the Apostle Paul is a harbinger of the later argument of Immanuel Kant. The most famous defense of the doctrine of the resurrection is found in 1 Corinthians 15.

Paul says in verses 12–13: "Now if Christ is proclaimed as raised from the dead, how can some of you say that there is no resurrection of the dead? But if there is no resurrection of the dead, then not even Christ has been raised." The Apostle is constructing a train of thought that is meticulously, and at times pedantically, logical. He moves from the universal to the particular, rigorously applying, in a manner that would delight Aristotle, the laws of immediate inference.

He says that if there is categorically no resurrection, then even Christ has not been raised. If Christ has not been raised, "then our preaching is in vain" (v. 14). How would you like to think that all the work you do is useless? What Paul says is that if Christ is not raised, then all the preaching of the Apostles was futile. It was done in vain. Not only

Paul's preaching, and the preaching of the other Apostles, but everyone's preaching is an exercise in futility.

Even further, Paul says that "your faith is in vain" (v. 14). This directly contradicts those who claim to have faith in Jesus but don't believe in a historical resurrection. If Christ is not raised, all religious faith and endeavor and significance is ridiculous. He goes on to say, "We are even found to be misrepresenting God, because we testified about God that he raised Christ, whom he did not raise if it is true that the dead are not raised" (v. 15).

This is impeccable logical progression. If the dead are not raised, then Christ has not been raised. If Christ has not been raised, our faith is in vain and we are still in our sins. Not only has our faith in Christ as our hope for eternal life vanished if there is no resurrection, but so also has our faith in Christ as Savior, because a dead Jesus can justify no one. For as Scripture says, Jesus was "raised for our justification" (Rom. 4:25).

Without the resurrection, the child, parent, spouse, or friend whom you committed to the earth with a wonderful religious service is gone. They have perished irrevocably. Then Paul says, "If in Christ we have hope in this life only, we are of all people most to be pitied" (1 Cor. 15:19). In other words, unbelievers should not be angry at Christians. Rather, they should pity us, for we are the most miserable of all people. We have committed ourselves body and soul to a false and fraudulent hope. If Christ is not raised, we are of all creatures the most miserable.

Notice that thus far in the text, Paul has said nothing different from what Kant would later say. However, the Apostle does not go on to say: "Therefore, believe in Christ. Take this leap into the dark and hope that Jesus came back from the dead, because if you don't believe it, we have no hope." That's not his argument. Rather, he says, "But in fact Christ has been raised from the dead, the firstfruits of those who have fallen asleep" (v. 20). At the beginning of this chapter, Paul says: "Now I would remind you, brothers, of the gospel I preached to you, which you received, in which you stand, and by which you are being saved, if you hold fast to the word I preached to you—unless you believed in vain. For I delivered to you as of first importance what I also received: that Christ died for our sins in accordance with the Scriptures" (vv. 1–3).

Paul pointed his readers back to the concrete, future historical prophecies that were written down not secretly but for the world to read, analyze, examine, and test. All can see how these specific, predictive prophecies were concretely and historically fulfilled perfectly in the life of Jesus of Nazareth. The Old Testament writers placed themselves in the empirical realm where their claims could be either verified or falsified, and we can look at the way that history vindicated the fulfillment of these predictions and see whether these writers were credible sources.

The first thing that Paul calls attention to is the Scriptures. This is not to say that he simply called people to believe just because the Bible says so. He wanted his readers to believe because of the empirical evidence and testimonies of people who had such a commitment to truth that they were prepared to die to defend it. Paul is speaking of something that was done publicly. "[Jesus] appeared to Cephas, then to the twelve. Then he appeared to more than five hundred brothers at one time, most of whom are still alive, though some have fallen asleep" (vv. 5–6). Five hundred eyewitnesses, and not one word is recorded from them denying this fact. Paul's original audience could have spoken in person with these witnesses, most of whom were still alive. When Paul stood before King Agrippa, he said: "For the king knows about these things, and to him I speak boldly. For I am persuaded that none of these things has escaped his notice, for this has not been done in a corner" (Acts 26:26).

And after Jesus had appeared to the five hundred, "he appeared to James, then to all the apostles. Last of all, as to one untimely born, he appeared also to me" (1 Cor. 15:7–8). Paul is not resting his faith on a deduction drawn from an empty tomb. It's not that the disciples went to the tomb, found it empty, and then began to speculate as to why the tomb was empty. They saw with their eyes and heard with their ears. Paul received their testimony, and he saw the resurrected Christ himself.

The fact that the Apostle Paul says that he saw the resurrected Christ does not in and of itself prove that Christ came back from the dead. What every Christian must answer is this: Do you trust this man? Do you trust Cephas? Do you trust the Twelve? Do you trust the five hundred? Do you trust the prophets? Do you trust the integrity of the most sacred historical witness that the world has ever known? Would such trust be reasonable or unreasonable?

Paul called himself "the least of the apostles, unworthy to be called an apostle, because I persecuted the church of God" (v. 9). In the midst of his skepticism and hatred and hostility toward Christianity, Paul saw the resurrected

Christ. At the end of the chapter, he says: "Why are we in danger every hour? I protest, brothers, by my pride in you, which I have in Christ Jesus our Lord, I die every day! What do I gain if, humanly speaking, I fought with beasts at Ephesus? If the dead are not raised, 'Let us eat and drink, for tomorrow we die'" (vv. 30–32). Ever since Paul saw Christ, his life became a living death. Why would Paul do that for a dead Jesus? He ends the chapter with this conclusion:

Behold! I tell you a mystery. We shall not all sleep, but we shall all be changed, in a moment, in the twinkling of an eye, at the last trumpet. For the trumpet will sound, and the dead will be raised imperishable, and we shall be changed. For this perishable body must put on the imperishable, and this mortal body must put on immortality. When the perishable puts on the imperishable, and the mortal puts on immortality, then shall come to pass the saying that is written: "Death is swallowed up in victory." "O death, where is your victory? O death, where is your sting?" The sting of death is sin, and the power of sin is the law. But thanks be to God, who gives us the victory through our Lord Jesus Christ. Therefore, my beloved brothers, be steadfast, immovable, always abounding in the work of the Lord, knowing that in the Lord your labor is not in vain. (vv. 51–58)

We are to be steadfast, immovable, abounding in the work of the Lord because not an ounce of that labor is wasted. Not a moment is futile because we have a Savior who says to us, "Forevermore." Christ has triumphed over the most obscene of all enemies, death. It was impossible for death to hold Him, for in Him is life itself. He is the Creator, Sustainer, and Redeemer of life, and He has willed the triumph of life. And He gives us grace to live and grace to die as people who trust in the promise of Christ.

Chapter Four

Living by Faith

We have already looked at the life of Abraham the patriarch as a vivid example of living by faith. We saw the historic moment in Genesis 15 where God made a covenant with Abraham, promising an heir even though he was advanced in years and his wife was barren and long past the age of childbearing.

When Abraham told his wife that she would conceive, Sarah laughed, as the prospect of her bearing a child was all but impossible. As Abraham awaited the fulfillment of

God's promise, he grew impatient and took matters into his own hands. A son was born through his wife's hand-maiden, Hagar, and the child was named Ishmael. But Ishmael was not the child of promise.

Finally, after much waiting and anguish, God fulfilled His promise. Sarah conceived and brought forth the son that Abraham had longed for, and they named him Isaac, which means "he laughs." Can you imagine the joy that Abraham experienced the day that Isaac was born? This was the child of promise. This was Abraham's heir, and through him all the nations of the world would be blessed.

As the story progresses, we see Abraham's journey of faith continue to unfold years later in Genesis 22, where he hears a voice calling his name and responds, "Here I am" (v. 1). God says to Abraham, "Take your son, your only son Isaac, whom you love, and go to the land of Moriah, and offer him there as a burnt offering on one of the mountains of which I shall tell you" (v. 2).

Notice how God speaks to Abraham. He is not vague, indefinite, or ambiguous. He does not simply tell Abraham to take his son to Mount Moriah and offer him on the altar. Had God done so, Abraham might have gone directly to Ishmael, not to Isaac. So God clearly says, "Take your son, *your only son Isaac*, whom you love." God wanted the child that Abraham dearly loved. In greatly understated terms, verse 3 then says: "So Abraham rose early in the morning, saddled his donkey, and took two of his young men with him, and his son Isaac. And he cut the wood for the burnt offering and arose and went to the place of which God had told him."

In his work *Fear and Trembling*, the poet and philosopher Søren Kierkegaard meditated on the significance of the words found in Genesis 22:3. With vignettes of insight, Kierkegaard speculated on why Abraham rose so early in the morning. The traditional answer we often hear is that Abraham was so committed to God, so strong in his faith, that he wanted to obey God's command as quickly as possible. In other words, the reason that Abraham rose early in the morning was so he could promptly carry out this command from God. However, that is not the most likely explanation of what was occurring in this narrative.

Sometimes we tend to turn biblical heroes and heroines into paper saints, into virtual characters of mythology. But Abraham was a man, just like you and me. He had the same fears, the same struggles, and the same anxieties that beset us. What would you do if God came to you and told you to take your only child and kill him or her? How would you sleep? Most of us have been in situations where we have something very important to do the following day, and in order to have the strength required, we know we need a good night's rest. But the more we know we need to sleep, the harder it is to sleep.

We wake up every fifteen minutes, look at the clock, and panic all the more. So finally, early in the morning, we give up and figure that we might as well get up because sleep is impossible. That's probably what happened to Abraham. He couldn't sleep knowing what was soon to unfold. So he rose early in the morning, saddled his donkey, took two young men and Isaac with him, and cut the wood for the burnt offering.

Abraham went to the place where God had told him, and on the third day he looked and saw the place from afar. As we read the story, it almost seems as though God was torturing Abraham. It would have been one thing for God to have told Abraham to kill his son immediately and have it done. But instead, He sent him on a journey. For three days, Abraham walked with his son. Finally, Abraham looked up, and in the distance he could see the slopes of Mount Moriah. We can only imagine what was going through his mind. The text tells us what happened next:

> Then Abraham said to his young men, "Stay here with the donkey; I and the boy will go over there and worship and come again to you." And Abraham took the wood of the burnt offering and laid it on Isaac his son. And he took in his hand the fire and the knife. So they went both of them together. And Isaac said to his father Abraham, "My father!" And he said, "Here I am, my son." He said, "Behold, the fire and the wood, but where is the lamb for a burnt offering?" (Gen. 22:5–7)

Isaac saw the firewood and the implement required to make a sacrifice, but the lamb that Isaac expected would be sacrificed was missing. At that moment, Abraham did not tell his son that Isaac himself was the sacrifice. Instead, he said, "'God will provide for himself the lamb for a burnt offering, my son.' So they went both of them together" (v. 8). All too often, the sermons preached on this passage make Abraham sickeningly pious, as though he wasn't a bit concerned about what was soon to transpire. But to live by faith means that sometimes we must hang on to a barren cliff with our fingernails as we try with all our strength to trust in an invisible God.

We don't know how the sacrifice unfolded, but we can imagine. As Isaac finally understood that he was to be the sacrifice, Abraham looked at his son, whose eyes were pleading with him, saying, "No, father!" Abraham took the knife and raised it, his trembling hand about to plunge the knife into the heart of his son. And at the last possible second, God called to him and said, "Abraham, Abraham! . . . Do not lay your hand on the boy or do anything to him, for now I know that you fear God, seeing you have not withheld your son, your only son, from me" (vv. 11–12).

Never in human history did a knife fall out of a man's hands so fast. He lifted up his eyes, and there was a ram, caught in the thicket by its horns—a ram that God provided for the ultimate sacrifice. Centuries passed as others tried to follow Abraham's example and live by faith, and another Father was placed in the same position. This Father took His Son, His only Son, the Son whom He loved, Jesus. God took His Son, bound Him, and prepared to sacrifice Him. But this time, no one cried out, "Stop!"

Jesus was sacrificed by the Father for us. God kept His promise and offered the sacrifice Himself so that we can live by faith. That is a God worthy of our trust. We cannot begin to imagine the cost of our redemption. Jesus drank the cup of God's wrath at sin—the whole cup, to the bitter dregs—so that we might have life and have it abundantly.

Chapter Five

Being Faithful

Romans 1:17 is often said to contain the thematic statement for the entire epistle of Romans: "For in [the gospel] the righteousness of God is revealed from faith for faith, as it is written, 'The righteous shall live by faith.'" Paul's letter to the church at Rome is also often said to represent his theological magnum opus. In this letter we find the most comprehensive and in-depth treatment of the central articles of our faith, not only among the writings of Paul but also in the entire New Testament. Therefore, we should pay close attention to the thematic statement that crystallizes the central focus of the book.

In this theme verse, Paul says that the righteousness of God is revealed by faith. This refers not to the righteousness by which God Himself is righteous but to the righteousness that is now made available to us by faith in Jesus Christ. At the end of this statement, the Apostle quotes the Old Testament, saying, "As it is written, 'The righteous shall live by faith.'" These words should occupy our attention not only because of their position in the thematic statement of Romans but also because this same verse is cited three times in the New Testament.

This quote originates in the book of the prophet Habakkuk, a prophet with a troubled spirit who lived and ministered to the people of Judah during one of the nation's darkest hours. Habakkuk lived in a time of judgment, during which God used pagan nations to implement His wrath and punishment against His own people.

This greatly perplexed the prophet, who couldn't understand why God would act in such a manner. Habakkuk built a watchtower, and there he wrestled with God, asking how He could let such atrocities happen to His people at the hands of an even more wicked nation. God is too holy to even behold iniquity, yet it seemed that He'd turned His back on His people, allowing wickedness to prevail in their midst.

Most of us understand what it's like to struggle with God and ask, "How can these things be?" It was in that context of doubt—doubt that pushed the prophet to the brink of despair—that the Word of God proclaimed, "The righteous shall live by his faith" (Hab. 2:4). It's almost as though in the midst of the dilemma, God didn't give a lengthy explanation for the intricacies of what He was doing in His sovereignty over world history. But He says to His prophet Habakkuk, "Trust Me."

There comes a time in every Christian's life when it seems that the only answer we get from heaven is God's response of "Trust Me." But what does it mean that the righteous shall live by faith? We could render the text this way: The righteous shall live by trust.

Unfortunately, it is rare in our day for Christians to ask how they might become more righteous. Pursuing righteousness is considered an old-fashioned idea that not many people consider. Christian bookstores are filled with books on self-improvement and how to be "spiritual," but biblically there's only one reason to cultivate spirituality: so that we become righteous. For the Christian, being spiritual, pious, moral, or ethical is never an end in itself. The goal of the Christian life is righteousness.

When we come to the New Testament, we hear the command to "seek first the kingdom of God and his righteousness, and all these things will be added to you" (Matt. 6:33). The pursuit of righteousness is a top priority with our Lord. Looking at it from another angle, Jesus said this: "For I tell you, unless your righteousness exceeds that of the scribes and Pharisees, you will never enter the kingdom of heaven" (Matt. 5:20).

What did Jesus mean? Many times these words don't disturb us as they should because of our understanding of the scribes and Pharisees. We are aware of their terrible hypocrisy and conclude that surpassing their righteousness is not at all difficult since they didn't seem to have much righteousness to begin with. But we need to take a closer look at the Pharisees to better understand Jesus' statement.

The Pharisees originally began as a group of Jews who were distressed by the creeping secularism of the nation of Israel. In response, they gathered together and devoted themselves to the singular task of being obedient to almighty God. They were the conservatives. They were the orthodox people of their society. With diligence and discipline, they studied the Scriptures day and night. They searched the Scriptures in a way that would shame many of us.

Jesus also spoke of how they tithed their mint and cumin. The Pharisees paid their tithes. That means they gave 10 percent of all they had to the work of God. But even with all this, Jesus denounced them for their lack of righteousness. He said that unless our righteousness exceeds the righteousness of the Pharisees, we will not enter the kingdom of God. That is a terrifying thought.

One way to understand Jesus' words is to say that we're justified by faith in Christ. After all, that is what the book of Romans is about. In faith, we have the righteousness of Christ Himself. We are clothed in Jesus' righteousness, and the merits of Christ far exceed all the collective merits and righteousness of all the Pharisees who ever lived. Therefore, in Christ we possess a righteousness that exceeds the righteousness of the scribes and Pharisees.

We are justified by faith, which means that we are justified by the righteousness of Christ. But the moment we are justified is only the beginning of the Christian life, and justified people are called to bring forth the fruit of our justification. We are called to conform to the image of Christ, to grow up into the likeness of Christ. In a word, we are called to produce the fruit of righteousness.

Luther said the believing sinner is *simul justus et peccator*—at the same time just and sinner. We are just by virtue of the righteousness of Christ, but in and of ourselves we are still sinners—sinners who, if we have true faith, are in the process of being sanctified and of bringing forth the fruit of righteousness. It cannot be a superficial righteousness, a righteousness that merely majors in externals like that of the Pharisees; instead, it must be a righteousness that penetrates the very core of our souls. The question is, Do we want to be righteous like that? If so, how can we be righteous?

The words of Scripture that tell us "the righteous shall live by faith" help us answer this question. If we want to be righteous, then we must understand what it means to trust God, who is altogether trustworthy. If we are to grow in righteousness, then we must grow in our capacity to trust God. We must trust Him in both life and death. We must trust His Word. We must trust that His laws are given not to torment us or rob us of happiness but as an expression of His wisdom and benevolence.

To be certain, there are many times when we don't understand how God's law could be the most humane, kind, or wise thing. That is precisely when we have to trust Him, confessing that while we do not understand certain elements of His law, we know that His law reflects His total and perfect wisdom, His kindness, and His love.

Every time we sin, we bring into question the wisdom and kindness of God. We say that we can't be happy unless we do that which we know God doesn't want us to do. We look at the law of God, and it conflicts with our interests, desires, and passions. When this happens, we don't trust God's law, and we don't trust and obey God. When we don't obey God, we are not righteous. This is why we need the redemption found in Christ—because all sin is ultimately a lack of trust in the character of God. "The righteous shall live by faith" means that we trust God, and that we trust Christ and Christ alone for our salvation.

We know that at the heart of Christianity lies this concept of faith. There's no salvation apart from trust. Trust is vital to the Christian life. It is crucially important for us to put our trust in God and in Christ. But there's another aspect that we must also consider: What are the implications of this text for how other people put their trust in us as Christians?

We have all been hurt at some point in our lives when someone that we trusted broke that trust. We often hear today about the importance of being open, honest, and vulnerable. But that is foolishness. We all know that we must be very careful with whom we discuss our innermost fears, failures, and sins because people disappoint us. Augustine wrote that one of the bitterest experiences he ever had was being betrayed by his closest friend. The truth is that there is no one we can trust completely except God. If we place our ultimate trust in human beings, then ultimately we will be disappointed.

We've all felt the pain of being let down by someone that we trusted. But sooner or later, we must realize that trust begins with us. When we stand before Christ at the end of our lives, the question we will have to deal with is not how many people let us down but rather how many people we let down and how many times we did not keep our word.

No wonder our Lord says, "Let what you say be simply 'Yes' or 'No'" (Matt. 5:37). Christian morality is not about whether we go to movies or dance. It is about righteousness—doing what is right. It is a question of integrity. What good is it if we have piety but our word means nothing? What good is it if we abstain from alcohol but don't pay our bills on time? Or if we say that we're going to be somewhere and don't go? Or that we're going to do something and we don't do it? That has no integrity.

I've heard it said so many times among Christians that they'd rather do business with pagans than with Christians because with pagans they know to be on guard, while Christians pray and smile while they break their contracts. But the righteous shall live by faith. The righteous shall live by trust. Their lives will be gripped by trust. Their lives will be characterized by trust. Not only do they trust God, but people can trust them. They can be trusted with a secret; they can be trusted to keep their promises and vows. Their yes means yes and their no means no.

The prophet Micah gave an excellent summary of the godly life when he answered the question, What does God require of us? If you're a Christian, you've asked that question. So often, people want to know how they can discern God's will for their lives. While it's impossible to get the kind of certainty we want in advance when it comes to things like where to live or whom to marry, we can know this with absolute certainty: the will of God for our lives is our sanctification (1 Thess. 4:3). If we make seeking the kingdom of God and His righteousness the main business of our lives, then we can have peace when it comes to our decisions about where to live or whom to marry.

The answer God gave in the book of Micah about what God requires of us is this: "to do justice, and to love kindness, and to walk humbly with your God" (6:8). To do justice is to do what is right. That is what God requires. To love kindness—this is the Hebrew word *hesed*, which is usually translated by the phrase "steadfast love," a term that characterizes God Himself. Our God is a God of steadfast love. Our God is a God of love whom we can trust.

What does God require of us? To do what is right, to love with loyalty, and to walk humbly with our God. That is the essence of the Christian life. That is the essence of what it means to live by faith.

God is altogether trustworthy. He has never told a lie; He's never broken a promise. He is loyal and steadfast to us, declaring that what He has begun in us He will finish (Phil. 1:6). He will stand with us and for us to the end. May we achieve the reflection of His character so that we might become mirrors of His righteousness—not in an attempt to be self-righteous or to gain heaven by our righteousness, but rather as a response to His righteousness. May we be trustworthy, because we of all people understand how precious trustworthiness is, because we have trusted God and His Son, our Savior.

About the Author

Dr. R.C. Sproul was the founder of Ligonier Ministries, founding pastor of Saint Andrew's Chapel in Sanford, Fla., first president of Reformation Bible College, and executive editor of *Tabletalk* magazine. His radio program, *Renewing Your Mind*, is still broadcast daily on hundreds of radio stations around the world and can also be heard online. He was the author of more than one hundred books, including *The Holiness of God*, *Chosen by God*, and *Everyone's a Theologian*. He was recognized throughout the world for his articulate defense of the inerrancy of Scripture and the need for God's people to stand with conviction upon His Word.